The Movement
Historical Changes During the Pandemic

About the Author

Robin Lewis has been painting and drawing for many years. For the past 15 years, she has written short poems and stories. Art and her children have been her inspiration for writing. She is passionate about a lot of things that inspire and positively change people.

Learn more about her at www.robinlewisart.com

ISBN 978-1-7362546-1-5
Copyrighted Material 2020 The Writers Pub

On September 1st, 2016, Colin Kaepernick kneeled on the football field during the national anthem to bring attention to racial inequality and police brutality. He kneeled specifically for the shooting death of Mario Woods, a black man, age 26 of San Francisco. Mario was shot 20 times by the police. While his actions may have inspired many and started a movement, he was shunned by the media and the NFL. Kaepernick was also banned from playing football.

COVID -19

COVID-19 was identified in January of 2020. COVID-19 is caused by a coronavirus called SARS-Cov 2. It is a virus that may start with flu-like symptoms. Some people say it's like having a cold, while others reported worse conditions that made them very sick for weeks. The virus can be contracted by air when a person breathes, coughs, sneezes, or talks, and it may stay on surfaces for up to three days. Close contact with infected individuals has caused the virus to spread rapidly. This virus has caused many deaths. It can infect anyone, but older people and immune compromised individuals are at greater risk. Scientists are working aggressively to develop a vaccine, but as of today, January 16th, 2020, only the symptoms can be treated.

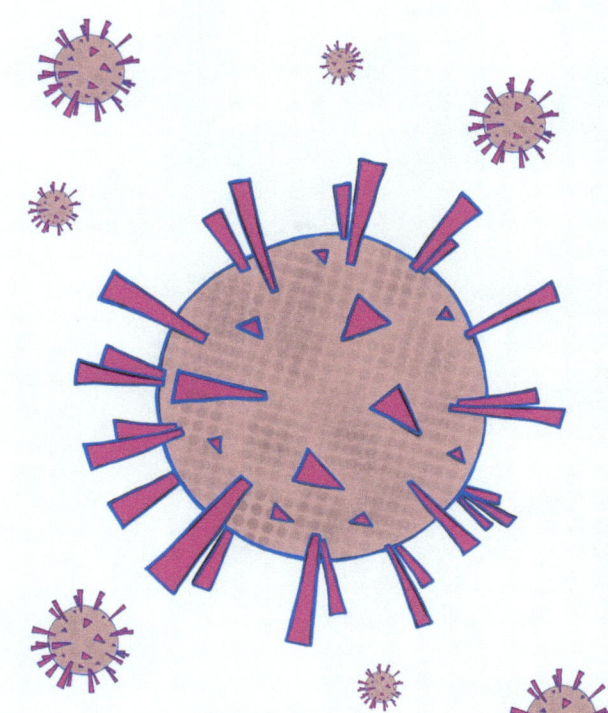

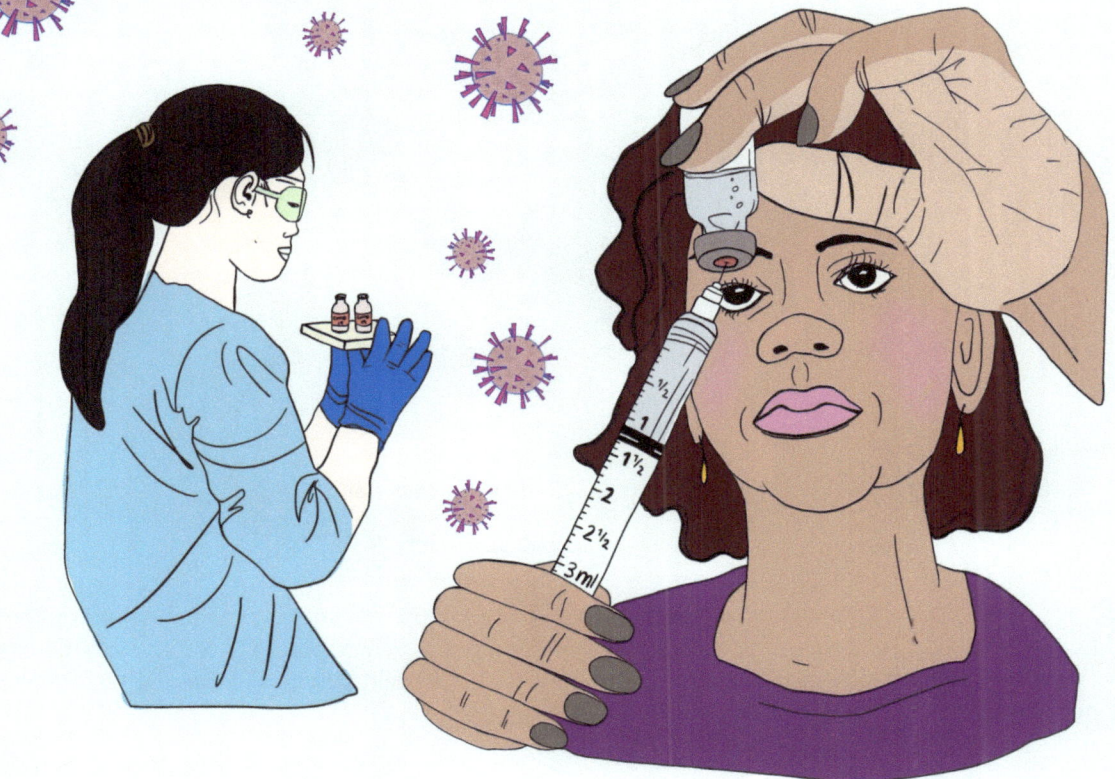

On February 23rd, 2020, Ahmaud Arbery, a 25 year old black man was shot and killed while jogging in a South Georgia neighborhood. The two white men that killed Ahmaud were not immediately arrested when it happened. The delayed investigation and slow arrest of the suspects received national attention. Ahmaud was an innocent black man just doing what he loved to do and that was to run.

On March 15th, 2020, Breonna Taylor, a 26 year old unarmed black female, was fatally shot at least 8 times by police in her Louisville, Kentucky, apartment. Breonna was a medical worker who also wanted to become a nurse; she loved helping people. Her death sparked protests in the United States and around the country.

COVID-19 cases in the United States March 2020

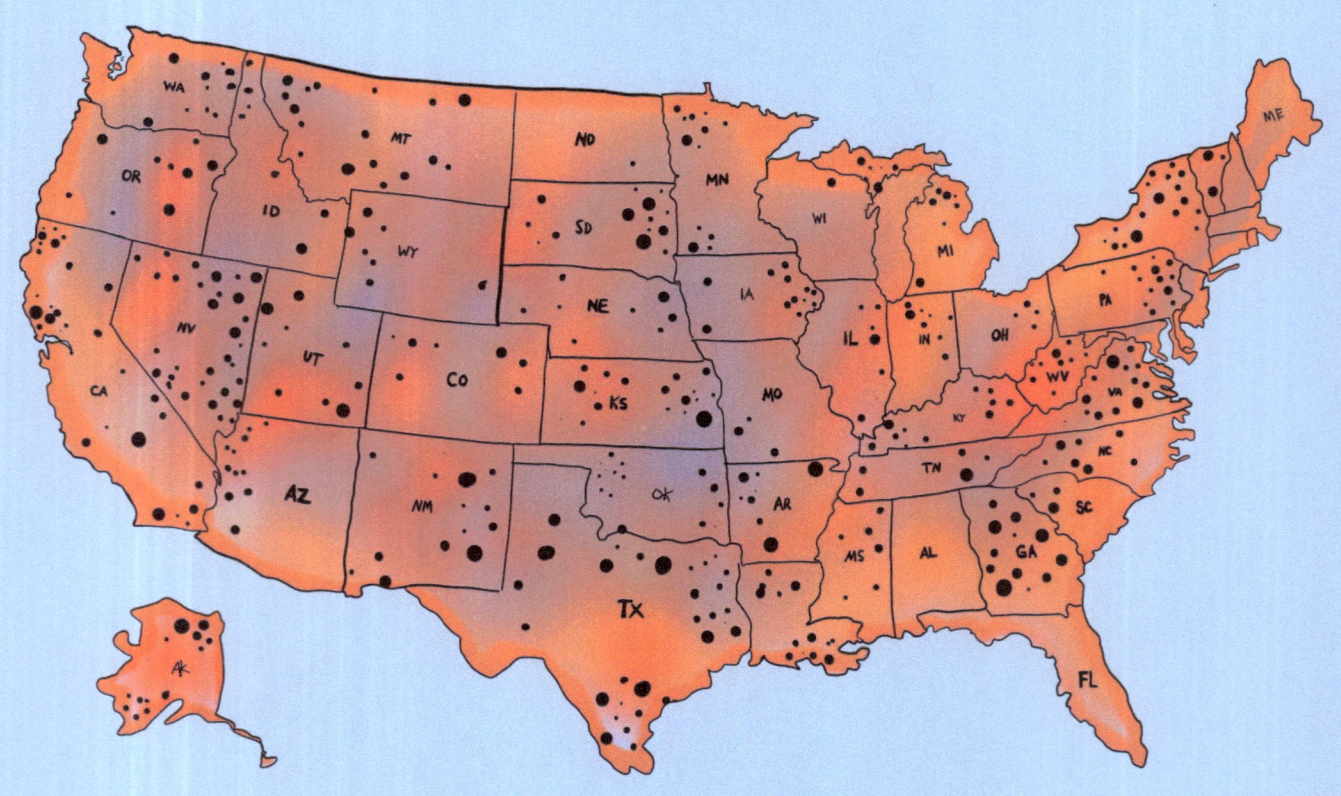

The COVID outbreaks increased more and more as the weeks passed. It was declared a pandemic in March of 2020 by the World Health Organization due to the speed of which it had spread globally. The United States alone had over 160,500 positive tests in the first week of March. China also confirmed an increase in cases to exceed over 89,000 and over 3,000 deaths around the same time. Many other countries including Iraq, France, Canada, Germany, Russia, and Morocco, all reported a spike in cases and COVID related deaths. The COVID-19 virus was all around the world.

Essential Workers
Save Lives

Doctors and Nurses

Grocery Clerk

Bus Driver

Since there was no vaccine or cure for COVID-19, distance and the wearing of masks when in contact with people became the normal. Masks were required to ride the bus, shop, go to the doctor's office and anywhere else. Services were denied for many people that did not wear a mask. Essential workers had to work long, hard hours during this difficult time; many of them were exposed to COVID-19.

Schools and colleges were closed temporarily, but over time closed for the remainder of the year due to an outbreak in COVID-19 cases and a reduction in staff when students returned to school. Virtual learning was the only option. Laptops were provided for each student so that they could interact with their teachers at home. Free meals were also available for many students to take home. It was a very difficult time for parents, staff members, and students.

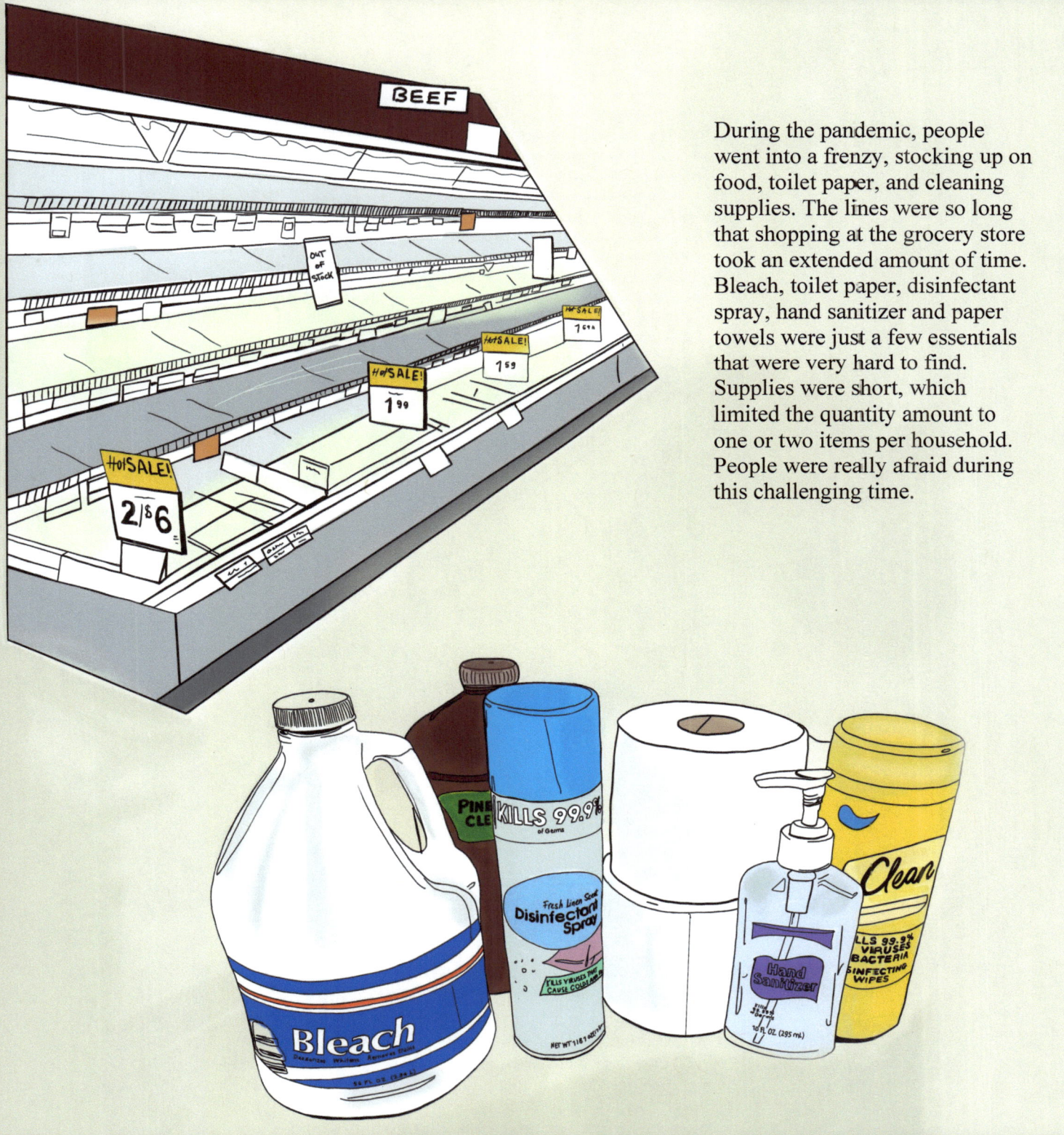

During the pandemic, people went into a frenzy, stocking up on food, toilet paper, and cleaning supplies. The lines were so long that shopping at the grocery store took an extended amount of time. Bleach, toilet paper, disinfectant spray, hand sanitizer and paper towels were just a few essentials that were very hard to find. Supplies were short, which limited the quantity amount to one or two items per household. People were really afraid during this challenging time.

In April of 2020, during the pandemic, the United States government put funds in place that assisted the American people. The government offered pandemic unemployment, which increased the unemployment payments to an additional $600 per week. Stimulus payments of $1200 per person were issued to working and non-working individuals and, additional food stamps were given each month to help families with food. The government also extended mortgage and rent payments for many months to prevent many people from losing their homes.

On May 8th, 2020, Ahmaud Arbery would've been 26 years old. Instead of celebrating, people jogged 2.23 miles all over the world, symbolizing the date of his fatal shooting while taking his last run. The amount of support from all around the country was amazing. Many people held up signs and posted the hashtags #IRUNWITHMAUD #RUNFORMAUD and #AHMAUDARBERY on their social status.

On May 25th, 2020, George Floyd was videotaped laying on the ground with a knee to his neck for eight minutes, by an on duty police officer. He died handcuffed while in police custody. His death ignited a massive movement across the country against systemic racism and police brutality.

Thousands of people were out of work. Schools and businesses were closed due to COVID-19, which created a lot of tension. Add the viral video death of George Floyd, and you have the ingredients for a perfect storm. People had more time to notice a lot of things that were happening. There was nowhere else to go, and people were just fed up. A lot of them took to the streets to protest against racial injustice and police brutality. They wanted their voices to be heard. They demanded a change.

The Black Lives Matter Plaza was created on June 5th, 2020, 11 days after George Floyd's death. The massive yellow and black mural was commissioned by Mayor Muriel Bowser of Washington DC. The mural is located in downtown DC North West and stretches two blocks. It was created by the DC public works department.

Each bright yellow letter is 35 feet tall and can be seen almost anywhere. Hundreds of people gather here every day. Since the unveiling of the mural, other cities participated by painting their own black lives matter murals, including the United Kingdom and Canada.

On June 8th, 2020, nine year old Kaitlyn Saunders, a figure skater, arrived at the Black Lives Movement Plaza. Kaitlyn skated on the painted pavement with her routine to the song "Rise" by Andra Day. Kaitlyn gained national attention; her idea was to replace negative messages with positive ones. She also wanted to inspire other black figure skaters and to give tribute to the Black Lives Matter Movement.

The Confederate General Robert E. Lee statue has stood in the center of Monument Avenue since 1890, in Richmond, Virginia. It stands 60 feet high. Since the movement addressing racial injustice and police brutality ignited by George Floyd's death, the statue has been spray painted and covered with words by protesters. On June 8th, 2020, the face of George Floyd was projected by Dustin Klein onto the base of the statue for all to see. Others who have died while in police custody have also been projected onto the statue.

Thousands of people protested for months. During this time, the faces of people killed by the police resurfaced again. Breonna Taylor and Ahmaud Arbery were among the many names mentioned during the movement. It wasn't just in the United States; many other countries joined in to protest for the victims and also use this time to fight for changes in their country. It was the largest global movement among people for change, and these things were taking place during the pandemic.

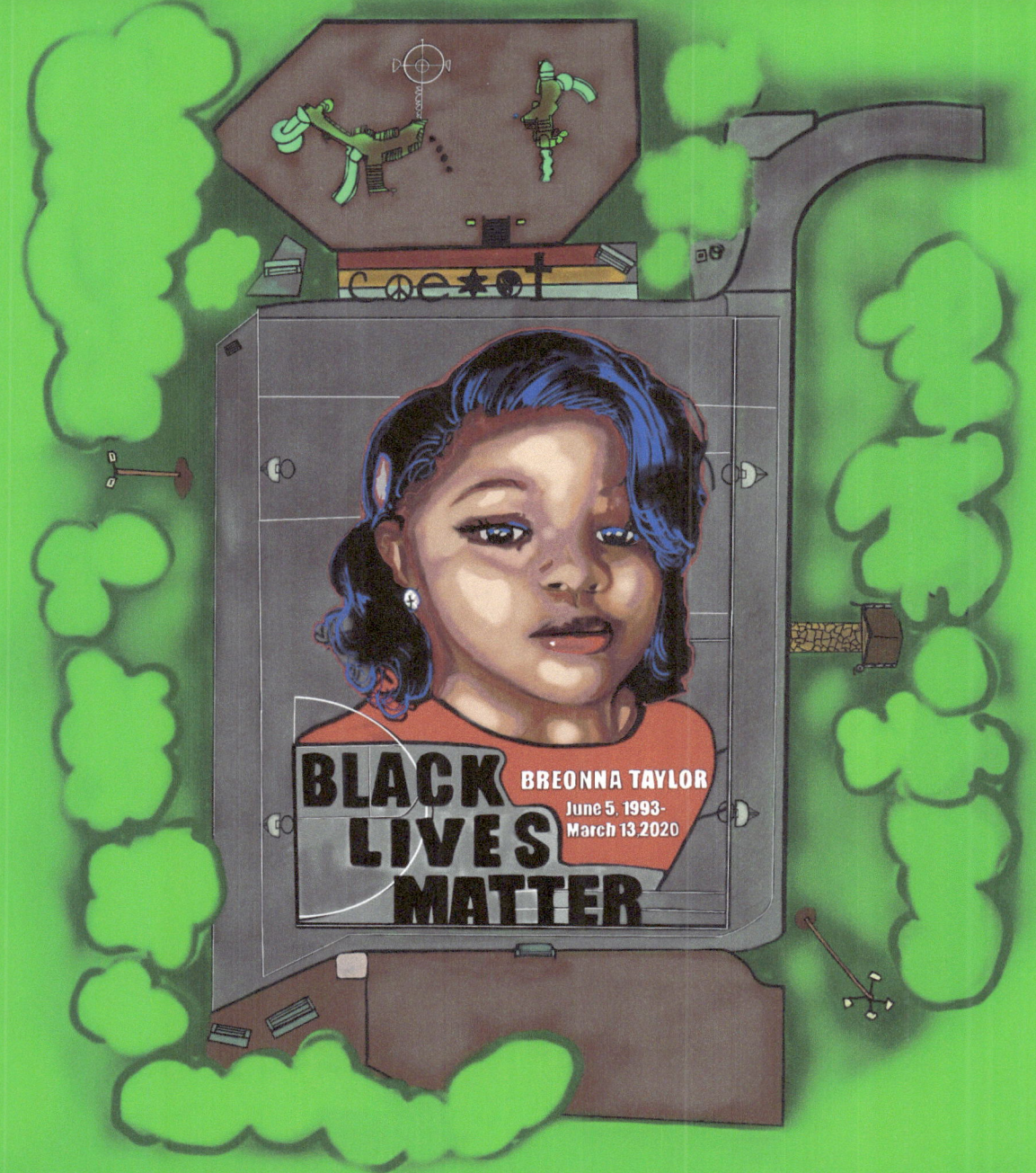

On July 5th, 2020, a 7,000 square foot mural of Breonna Taylor was created in Annapolis, MD in a historically black neighborhood. The mural was painted on the asphalt basketball courts in Chambers Park by 10 teaching artists, 15-20 youths, and 40 volunteers. They completed this large mural in 24 hours. The mural was painted as a tribute to Breonna Taylor and to bring attention to the prejudicial violence of African American women. The project was led by "Future History Now", in partnership with Banneker Douglass Museum and the Maryland Commission on African American History and Culture.

In July of 2020, Many of the Major League Baseball players used their platforms in support of the movement. They also wore the victims names on their shirts. This movement was so huge among the players from the different leagues. Everyone was unified and kneeling during the national anthem to end police brutality and racial injustice.

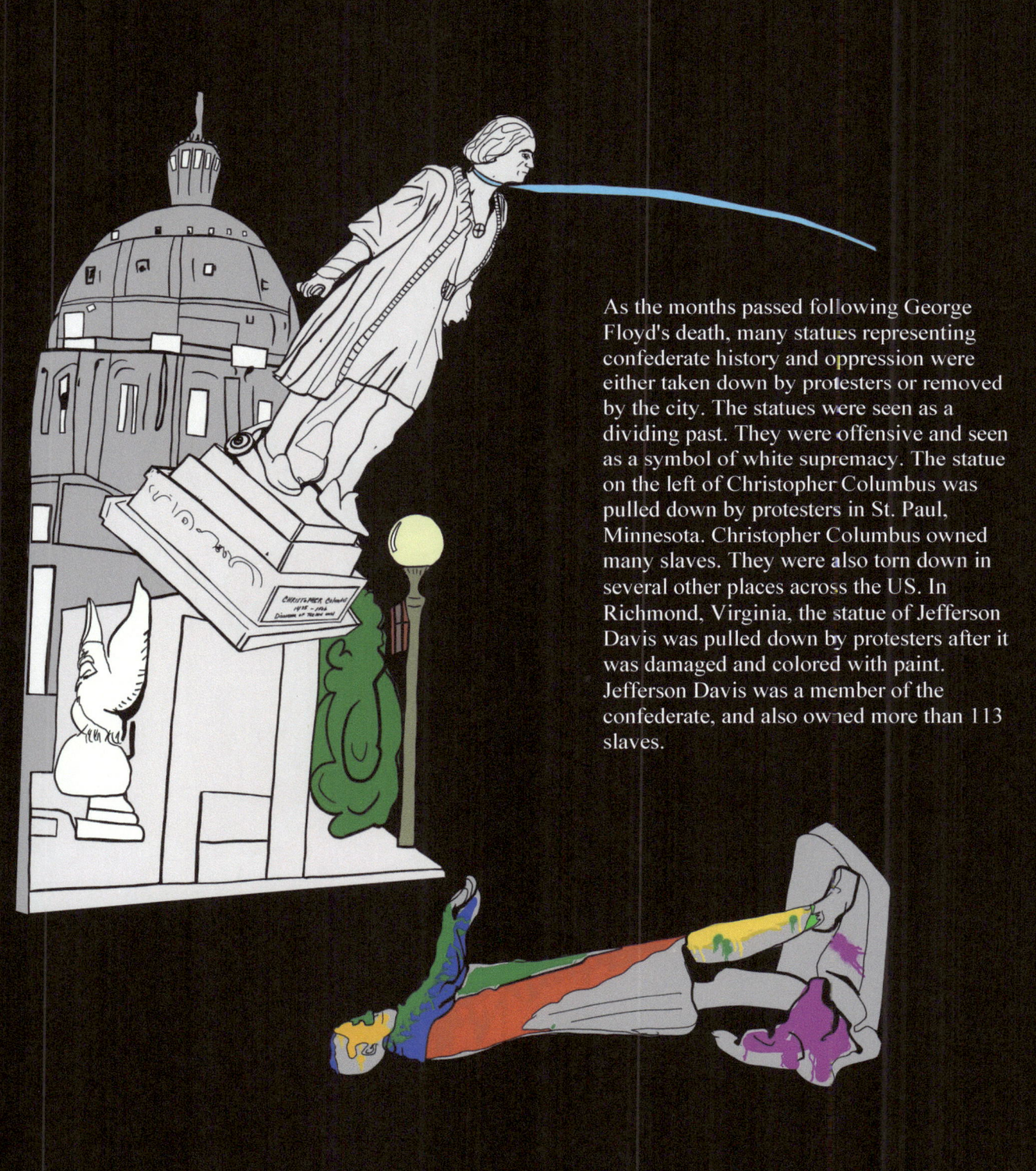

As the months passed following George Floyd's death, many statues representing confederate history and oppression were either taken down by protesters or removed by the city. The statues were seen as a dividing past. They were offensive and seen as a symbol of white supremacy. The statue on the left of Christopher Columbus was pulled down by protesters in St. Paul, Minnesota. Christopher Columbus owned many slaves. They were also torn down in several other places across the US. In Richmond, Virginia, the statue of Jefferson Davis was pulled down by protesters after it was damaged and colored with paint. Jefferson Davis was a member of the confederate, and also owned more than 113 slaves.

21

In August 2020, NBA players continued to use their platform for change by sitting out practices and games to take a moment to focus. Other leagues, such as the MLB and the NFL, were doing the same. During the days and weeks that followed, team members and coaches became unified in taking a stand against racial injustice and police brutality by also taking a knee during the national anthem. Many of the players and team members also displayed victims names and wore statements on their shirts and jerseys during the game.

NFL players used their platform to support the Black Lives Movement and to stand up for racial injustice and police brutality. They took a kneel during the national anthem. Coaches and team members also joined in to support the other players. Some of the NFL players displayed the victims names on the padding at the bottom of their helmets.

As the COVID-19 virus surged and deaths worldwide increased, the government issued mandatory shutdowns of salons, schools, churches, and many other places where people gathered. Many restaurants only offered delivery or pick-up for food. The buses were free to ride in some places for some time with a limited number of passengers. Some states had temporary curfews for their residents to keep social distancing in place. If you were out after curfew, you might be faced with a large fine for breaking the rules.

Today, December 11th, 2020, we have a vaccine that scientists are aggressively waiting to distribute. We are still fighting against racial injustice and police brutality. Together we stand not divided by gender, race, religion, color, ethnicity, or social status, but as people. Everyone has a voice to make positive changes through art, music, speech, dance, and other creative ideas. All people deserve inclusion, equality, and justice. Having a vaccine may treat COVID-19, but it does not treat racism or police brutality. We must work together to make the world we live in a better place for the generations to come. Be The Change You Want to See.

The Movement
Historical Changes During the Pandemic

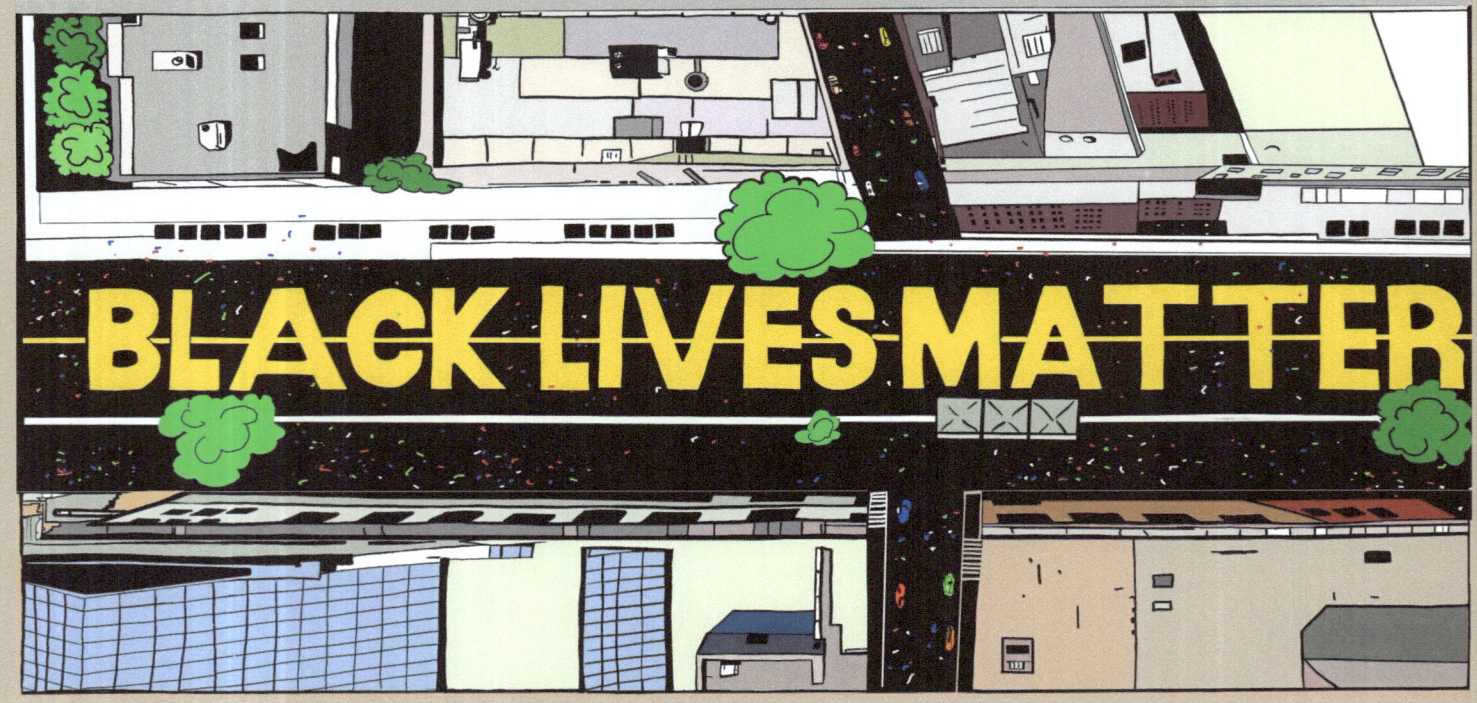

coloring books and reading books available

The Writers Pub   PO Box 74421   North Chesterfield Virginia 23236

www.robinlewisart.com

Copyrighted Material 2020 The Writers Pub